The Warrior's Journey

Ancient Wisdom For The Modern Entrepreneur

Megan Nolan

Contents

A Word of Thanks...

What a fun and wild experience it has been bringing this book to life! I want to give a deep heartfelt thanks to all the people that have helped me to bring this dream to life. I couldn't have done it without you.

Deep bows of gratitude to:

My partner, my GM, my love Justin who has been my #1 fan, always encouraging me. Reminding me to keep my chin up and stay positive, you've weathered many storms with me so elegantly.

My Seastar and my bestest friend in the world Liz Nolan. Who happens to be a front line health care Warrior who works tirelessly in service to others. I love you as wide as the sky.

My many coaches who've been my guides on this journey of creating and growing a business: Kimi Morton, James Wedmore, Christine McIver, but especially to Tony Babcock. Thank you Tony for walking alongside me with kindness and patience to remind me of who and what I really am.

My many Yoga teachers (a few of whom were mentioned in the book) who have gifted me with your knowledge and helped me to swim in the great ocean that is Yoga.

My book coach Anza Goodbar who so generously shared your insights, many strategies, and countless hours to give this book the life and reach it has.

My sweet editor Danielle Hines who gently taught me that CAPITALIZING words constantly is not needed for effect...LOL. You did such a brilliant job in smoothing out the edges of this book into what it is now. Thank you!

My loving friends, family, and community that cheered me on, near and far. Thank you so much for supporting me all along the way in my many ventures and adventures.

Finally, to you my beautiful reader, I am deeply grateful and honored that you're making the space in your life to explore this book with curiosity and an open heart.

Thank you for allowing me to be part of your Warrior's Journey.

I love you all,

A Blessing on Your Journey

May you always remember your true nature...

I stood with my feet planted on the earth, closed my eyes, and breathed deeply.

From the depths of my heart, I heard the universe whisper to me:

"Do you hear the roaring sound of the ocean?" You have that same power within you.

"Do you see the mist carried far on the wind?" Your magic travels the same way and reaches much farther than you know.

"Do you hear the birds singing their beautiful song?" Your heart sings those same songs of joy.

"Do you see those big, heavy rocks?" You have that same strength, steadiness, and resiliency.

"Do you see the spider's intricate web?" You too are woven into the web of life and are eternally supported.

"Do you see the butterfly dancing in the wind?" Your soul dances with that same lightness.

With another breath, the universe whispered: *"May you always remember your true nature little one: powerful, magical, joyful, strong, resilient, connected, supported, playful, and expansive."*

The same is true for you too my friend, and it's my intention that this book is a loving reminder of that.

Introduction

I believe that every human being is given a soul mission. As you travel through life it's up to you to discover it, nurture it, and let it be fully expressed through you.

In my humble opinion, this is even more true for those brave among us who decide to follow the path of entrepreneurship.

As an entrepreneur, there is a calling in your heart beckoning you to use your gifts and passions to serve your community. A quiet voice whispering to you about possibilities as it encourages you to breathe life into something that didn't exist before—your business. What a blessing!

The real truth is: entrepreneurship is not for the faint of heart. If anyone has sold you on the idea that running a business will be easy, sadly they were pulling your leg.

It is not a simple task to ride the emotional rollercoaster of business ownership. The unpredictability of the ups and downs is no joke, but wow is it worth it.

The funny thing is, and you'll likely agree, entrepreneurship is probably the ongoing, realtime lesson in personal development that you didn't know you needed. Am I right?

The vast number of things you go through in building and growing a business is almost indescribable. The to-do list is miles long and there's always something you could be doing....

Just when you think you've got things under control the universe takes you through that upside-down part of the rollercoaster where you feel like you may actually throw up and lose your shit for real this time....

Then the ride smooths out, maybe a launch goes well, you get a nice review on your podcast or a sweet DM. Life feels like sunshine and butterflies again, making you want to sing from the rooftops about how awesome and fulfilling owning a business is. Oh, happy day!!

The highs and lows are real. And after seventeen years of being in business for myself, I've come to recognize that there are invisible tools of success that aren't well -known.....until now.

Beyond the necessary strategies for business-building like social media tactics, email list, community growth, and everything in between, there are intrinsic qualities that you'll need to accomplish your beautiful soul's calling.

These powerful ways of being will send you charging after your mission as the brave Warrior you are and help you create the impact and income you dream of.

I only discovered them for myself a few years ago when I was at rock bottom in my life and really struggling in my business. And I am so grateful I did because they have changed everything for me.

Curious about what these essential tools are? Of course, you are!

Let's dive in so you can learn how to fully activate and embody them on every level of your being.

Here we go...

Chapter One

Before we move forward let's take a look back...

Before we go any further, I think giving you some context on what inspired this book would be best. To provide you with this insight, I'd like to take you back 6 years ago to when I found myself lying on my Yoga mat curled up in a crumpled heap on the floor in a puddle of tears...again.

At the time, I was working around the clock trying to help someone else grow their business and get my own going. I was utterly exhausted but could barely sleep because my body was aching in so much pain that I couldn't get comfortable in any position. So yes, it was rough, to say the least.

I spent my days frantically trying to move forward and get things done, which made it look like I was doing things and making progress. However, on the inside, I was either so anxious that I felt like a kite getting frantically whipped around in a tornado or I was consumed by so much doubt that I felt like I was crumbling under the weight of sadness and fear.

I really had no sense of joy or excitement about anything I was doing. I felt numb. I felt empty inside, completely drained of drive or desire to be doing what I was doing anymore.

I was literally pouring all of myself into my work, but it felt like it was just draining out the bottom. I felt empty, hollow, and as though I had nothing left to give.

Maybe you remember Eeyore from the children's series *Winnie the Pooh* written by A.A. Milne? He was the depressed donkey that plodded around sadly, dropping negative comments about everything.

He is not exactly the happiest character in the crew, but I felt like him on the darkest day he had. To make matters even worse, I felt like that almost every day.

On the morning that changed everything, I was in my usual spot laying on my Yoga mat and crying. Because I was so tapped out mentally and physically, this was my practice at the time. And this bothered me because I felt like a total fraud. A Yoga teacher that couldn't even really practice, a personal trainer that didn't even exercise—some model of health I was.

As I lay there, staring off into space spinning in the usual gamut of worry spirals in my head a leaf caught my eye. It was caught on a spider web, dangling by a thread, and getting tossed around wildly by the wind.

As the wind picked up and it was whipped up into a frenzy I realized that the leaf and I were both in the same situation:

Going in every direction but getting nowhere.

Working hard with not much to show for it.

Barely holding on by a thread.

In that moment as I felt my chest tightening and my stomach flipping with anxiety I literally felt myself crumbling into pieces. Looking back now, I likely was having a mild panic attack but who really knows?

The reality was, I had been through very tough times before, but I had never been at such a low point in my life. At that moment my heart started racing yet I felt frozen inside in an eerily calm state.

My body was numb, and my mind was suddenly so still for a change, and that's when I heard the quiet voice of my heart whisper softly:

"This isn't your path. You can't go on like this. You're a Warrior; you'll find a way."

Of course, the negativity committee in my head instantly piped in with all sorts of comebacks:

"You've made commitments, you can't just back out."

"You've done so much already, are you just gonna give up and quit?"

"You're a Warrior? What the heck does that even mean?"

"Some Warrior you are. Look at the mess you're in"

Having heard more than enough nonsense from my mind at that point, I yelled out: *"STOP!!"* to no one in particular, but clearly, I really needed to proclaim it.

The line in the sand had been drawn, and the words I heard became my battle cry as I lay there repeating my heart's guidance over and over:

"This is NOT my path. I will NOT go on like this. I am a WARRIOR. I will find a better way."

Inspired by this insight, I gradually set off on a journey to understand what this message meant so I could live this guidance.

Not being exactly sure where to start, I decided to re-introduce myself to the only Warriors I knew at the time, the ones I had met on the Yoga mat.

My complete lack of energy meant I wasn't really up for much of the physical practice of the poses, so instead, I decided to dive into the ancient myth that inspired them. Which interestingly enough, I had only heard for the first time days before. Little did I know that it would become the most powerful and life-changing of stories for me and hundreds of other people—including you!

The wild tale of the Warrior behind the poses is one of resilience, courage, determination, strength, and commitment. The story itself is rich with lessons and metaphors and tells the story of a Warrior named Virabhadra who is sent on a mission against the most challenging of opponents: his own mind.

Interestingly, the many twists and turns the tale takes have much to teach about the poses, the Yoga practice, and ultimately about your own journey of charging forward on your soul's mission!

As I dove into this ancient tale and the rich meaning behind it, I began to recognize how much more the tools of Yoga have to offer each of us....that is if you're open to them.

The truth is, despite what you see in the contortionist photos on social media, the real magic of the practice is what it awakens within you and what it helps you to become. This is beautifully explained by one of the modern masters of Yoga B.K.S. Iyengar who summed it up as: *"Yoga doesn't just change the way you look at things, it changes the one who sees."*

Day by day, breath by breath, the journey of awakening the Warrior within me began. As my energy returned, I would stand in the poses and recognize the resiliency of my mind, body, and spirit. Each time I stepped onto the mat, the poses activated even more focus, awareness, and power within me than I had ever felt before.

Slowly, the tiny spark turned to a flicker, then to a flame which ignited the deep knowing and confidence that I had not only found my path but could now light the way for others to do the same.

So, the moment that started as a dark night of my soul has since become my greatest teacher and a potent reminder of what is possible for all of us when we're willing to listen to the guidance of our heart.

That quiet voice inside will always help you navigate toward your purpose and potential so that you too can live into your soul's mission!

Within this book are the tools that you can use to come home to yourself and achieve the success and impact that you are destined for. Their versatility means you can use them to navigate the crazy, unpredictable nature of entrepreneurship and pretty much anything life throws at you.

Truthfully, I don't know where or who I'd be without them, nor do I really even want to know.

In hindsight, while that time in my life was extremely challenging, it is also the most rewarding because of the transformation it catalyzed within me and how it has propelled me forward.

So whether you're looking to learn more tools to use on your life's journey or you've reached a juncture in your life that has caused you to say your variation of:

"This is NOT my path. I will NOT go on like this. I am a WARRIOR, I will find a better way."

I'm deeply honored and grateful that you're here.

I hope this book gives you hope, inspires you, and awakens the Warrior within you.

My intention is that it sparks the fire of the beautiful light within you brightly so that you charge bravely forward toward your soul's mission like the unstoppable force you truly are.

So, are you ready to hear the story of Virabhadra the ancient Warrior that has many lessons to teach you about yourself, life, entrepreneurship, and everything in between?

Let's go!

Chapter Two

The why behind the Warrior....

Many people are surprised to learn that a soothing and relaxing practice like Yoga contains poses named after a Warrior. Especially when they hear that the Warrior has a thousand heads and a thousand arms each one carrying a sword.

While it may seem strange to include such a ferocious creature, when you consider that Yoga is based on Buddhism and Hinduism which each have many parables and teachings on life, it makes perfect sense. The ancient stories that inspired the poses are rich with meaning and were traditionally told within the practice to guide the student to a deeper understanding of the pose.

So what inspired me to weave this crazy story into a book about entrepreneurship? Well, consider that on a daily basis as an entrepreneur you:

- Face challenges that you need to make your way through

- Are called to use your tools to carve out a path for yourself to get to your goals

- Have a fire within you that sparks your expansion and growth, and spurs you on

It probably won't surprise you to learn that these same experiences are all expressed in the Warrior story as well as in the Yoga practice!

If you're willing to stay open and curious, these ancient teachings are also very applicable to your modern life. Because despite what you may have seen on social media, Yoga is actually a practice of you evolving into a fuller expression of yourself—not just trying to contort yourself into a *Cirque du Soleil* pretzel (unless that's your jam).

Before I introduce you to the wild, dreadlock-rocking Warrior named Virabhadra who inspired the iconic poses and this whole book, I want to mention that this isn't your average run-of-the-mill fairytale. It's actually nowhere close to that.

Instead, it's the tale of Shiva, a Hindu God who loses his temper in a wild fit of rage and creates the Warrior to avenge the loss of his true love and life partner, a human woman named Sati. It's full of fiery emotions, revenge, and fierce courage, but aren't the best stories kind of crazy? I mean, that's why we love them so much!

So consider yourself warned. After all, it is a metaphor for the challenging battle that we all face, learning to conquer the most difficult of opponents, your mind.

This story begins, as many good ones do, with two passionate lovers. Shiva and Sati have adored each other for lifetimes and have a beautiful life together.

Shiva is a wild and crazy God who is known for his destructive ways and wild temper. He loves to spend centuries sitting in meditation covered in ash with long wild dreadlocks.

Sati is a magnificent human who is the epitome of grace, gentleness, and beauty. While they are deeply happy with each other, her father Daksha despises the whole situation. To prove this, he decides to throw a party and invite the whole community....except for Shiva and Sati.

Deeply offended, Sati tries to rally Shiva to go with her to confront her father. Unphased and uninterested, Shiva decides to skip the party, preferring instead to settle in for a relaxing meditation.

Getting more annoyed by the minute, Sati goes to the party alone and marches right up to her father to explain how she feels. With all eyes on the two of them, Daksha seizes the opportunity to explain loudly why they can't be together and why Shiva isn't the one for her.

The conversation quickly escalates to a heated argument which causes Sati to lose her temper, burst into flames, and crumble to a pile of ashes on the floor.

The whole party sees this, and everyone is shocked.

Meanwhile, atop Mount Kalish, his favorite meditation place, Shiva instantly knows what has happened and flies into a devastated and infuriated rage. He yanks out one of his dreadlocks, throws it to the ground and creates Virabhadra: a powerful and ferocious Warrior with a thousand heads and a thousand arms, and charges him with his mission: *"Bring me Daksha's head!"*

So Virabhadra sets off, carving his way down the mountain, tunneling his way through the underground towards Daksha's palace.

Before you throw the book down in wonder of what the heck you've got yourself into, let me pause and remind you the story is a metaphor.

Through the characters and their experiences, the story explores the many aspects of you so that you may begin to learn more about yourself.

Take for example the deep love between Shiva and Sati. I'm willing to bet you have experienced a heart-felt love for a partner, friend, relative, or pet.

Or what about how both Shiva and Sati lose their temper?

Perhaps there is a passionate side of you that feels very strongly about certain things or sometimes causes you to lose your cool and burst into fiery emotion from time to time.

Each of the characters and the journey that Virabhadra is about to embark on has something to teach you. Plus they give you the chance to reflect on the wide spectrum of the human experience like intense love, gratitude, sadness, motivation, and more.

Through it all, the thread that weaves it together is Virabhadra. He is created and charged with a mission to return with Daksha's head. Metaphorically this represents the journey of Yoga: learning to quiet and focus your mind.

Ultimately, this is the journey that we're all on: learning to make your mind your friend, rather than your foe. Which of course is incredibly invaluable for everyone, but especially for you as an entrepreneur.

The truth is, as you put yourself out in the world and do things that place you in the spotlight your mind will do everything in its power to stop you and keep you safe.

You can't blame it though. After all, it's just trying to keep you in your comfort zone of familiarity. But as you already know, all of the amazing things you desire and see for yourself lie just beyond that boundary in the realm of the unknown and unfamiliar.

So that means it's essential that you get your mind on board and use it to your advantage so that you can learn to think on purpose, take inspired action, and accomplish the mission that your soul was given.

So are you ready?

Let's join Virabhadra the Warrior in the first part of his journey and see what tools he has to help you navigate your obstacles and challenges with as much grace and ease as possible.

Let the journey begin...

SECTION ONE: THE JOURNEY BEGINS

Charged with his mission Virbabhadra sets off, tunneling his way down through Mount Kalish and underneath the city towards the palace.

Imagine the darkness of his situation, creating a tunnel to make his way toward his goal. To get there he has to use his swords to carve his way through the many twists and turns.

He keeps his sights fixed forwards and upwards to propel himself towards his target. He is determined in his focus and courageous in his resiliency. Through it, he cultivates a deeply grounded self-awareness.

Can you see yourself in this at all as an entrepreneur?

Think back to when you first heard the calling in your heart to go into business for yourself.

Either you jumped right in and got started or took your time perhaps putting it off until the nudges to take action became so loud they were hard to ignore.

And off you went: unsure of exactly where you were heading but courageous enough to try.

Sharpening your skills and honing your craft along the way as you move towards your goal, just like Virabhadra is doing.

This part of the story has much to teach you about cultivating the tools of resilience, groundedness, and self-awareness which are key for navigating your journey.

So let's dive into these powerful tools!

Chapter Three

You've Got Bouncebackability

Been there, done that, got the T-shirt. Or so the saying goes, right?

The fact that you are here, reading this book tells me a lot of things:

1. You have AH-mazing taste in literature.

2. You're an entrepreneur, and that makes me like you even more. Or you're not, and instead, you're a friend or family member reading this out of love for me and guess what I love you right back.

3. You want to learn how to stoke the fire of the light within you so you can shine even brighter and that makes me tear up with joy. No joke, it really does.

But all of those fun facts about you aside, the fact that you're here tells me that you are resilient. You know: the pick yourself up and dust yourself off and keep going kind of person. My kind of person.

You've made it through some tough stuff. You've seen some crazy things. And you kept going. That deserves some big props and a million gold stars.

Because if there's one quality that is essential for an entrepreneur it's *resilience*.

While Oxford Dictionary defines it as:

"The capacity to recover quickly from difficulties, toughness"

OR

"The ability of a substance or object to spring back into shape, elasticity"

I define it as bounce-back-ability: your ability to weather the storm and emerge on the other side a different version of yourself. One that has been shaped by the experience, no longer the same, but back up on your feet and continuing on.

Because the truth is, despite what you may see on social media, entrepreneurship is no walk in the proverbial park.

There will be moments that take you to your knees and ones that follow that threaten to keep you there.

Times when you wonder what the heck possessed you to want to work for yourself and others that make you want to sing from the rooftops about the glory of being self-employed.

The ups are exhilarating, and the downs can be heavy.

But the common thread is YOU. You're the one that kept on keeping on. Bravo.

That is resiliency. To be honest, there have been times when my ability to keep going has surprised me.

Like teaching "group" Yoga classes with one student.

Or posting content to an audience of crickets.....I just kept going.

Like I did when a few years ago I was approached to teach live-streamed Yoga classes from the beach. This is really not surprising given that I live in one of the most beautiful places in the world, Maui, Hawaii.

Excited about the opportunity, I said yes and went for it. Yoga on the beach is lovely and sounds really glamorous until Mother Nature made her presence known and the blazing hot sun caused my phone to overheat and turn off midstream.

Unphased, I tried again with the phone tucked safely in the shade. Then a gust of wind blew up knocking my tripod over causing my phone to face-plant into the sand and water.

Running over to rescue it, I squatted down and flashed everyone who was still watching the live stream. Needless to say, the live streams didn't last much longer before they went with someone else.

However, it turns out that it was all part of the divine plan that was preparing me for something much bigger.

A few years later, I was contracted to teach an outdoor virtual Yoga session for a major telecommunications company as part of their team PRIDE celebrations. It was so fun and a total honor to be a part of!

On the day of the event, I arrived at the filming location to find a wedding happening. Obviously, this was not part of the original plan. Luckily, I had the foresight to have a plan B, so I headed up there to set up as quickly as I could.

As I tried to connect to their streaming platform we soon realized we had a major tech issue which meant another massive pivot was needed since we were due to start in just minutes.

Thankfully, the nail-biting moments of tech limbo didn't last too long (seriously don't they feel like hours) and we were off the races! Let the relaxation begin.

Luckily, my camera was tucked under the awning of the building (thanks past me who learned that lesson already!) because moments later, it began to rain. Which in Hawaii can either go two ways: a lovely soft mist or a blasting wind and rain so strong it can't help but remind you that you are, in fact, out in the middle of the ocean.

So there I am, decked out in a fabulous rainbow ensemble getting blessed by the Hawaiian rain Gods. Not a big deal, I've taught Yoga in the rain before. I'm rolling with it, and I begin guiding the class into Eagle pose when, out of nowhere, a Myna bird (a Hawaiian crow) comes flying right at me.

Side note, I'm terrified of birds thanks to my parents taking me to see Alfred Hitchcock's movie *The Birds* in 3D when I was five years old.

Time slowed down to a stop as he swooped right beside me and pooped right on my Yoga mat before he continued on! It was pure hilarity that I couldn't have even made up if I tried.

But though it all I just smiled, laughed, and blew them all away.

Because everything I had been through had prepared me for that moment.

Just like how everything that you have been through has shaped you into the you that you are right now. Very Dr. Seuss-esque, right?

The truth is, we will all get knocked down, but your ability to bounce back from it depends on a few factors.

First and foremost is the meaning that you give to the event. Do you define it as a colossal failure or part of the process that is helping you to grow?

Learning to reframe "failure" was one of the biggest keys to this for me. As someone who grew up being taught to value hard work and achieving my goals, the times when I didn't were difficult for me at first. I was hard on myself in these moments, and I critiqued everything.

I can vividly recall a time when my promotional launch didn't go as planned, and my coach asked me what I could celebrate about it and my answer was a harsh: *"Nothing."*

As far as I was concerned I didn't get to the finish line, so I didn't deserve any accolades.

Thankfully, she helped me to take a step back and witness everything that I had accomplished and all the lessons I had learned. Although I hadn't reached the goal, the whole experience was an incredible growth opportunity.

So what if you learn to see these times in your life the same way? One of my coaches James Wedmore sums this up very succinctly by saying: *"Either you'll get the results you want or the lessons you need."* Powerful right?

Choosing to see everything you go through along the way as happening FOR you rather than TO you is a very empowering perspective to take. This subtle but truly profound shift will help you to see perceived obstacles or problems in a totally new way—as tools to help you to become the version of you that you need to be to accomplish your mission.

Think about how this shows up on your Yoga mat when you're doing balance poses.

Let's say you're in a class and your teacher invites you to do Tree pose. So there you are, foot planted to the floor, other leg bent out to the side doing a pretty darn awesome Palm Tree impression.

A couple of deep breaths in and you're doing your best to stay steady but soon you find yourself swaying all over the place like a tree in a Hawaiian rain storm. For many people, this can be a huge source of frustration and cause all sorts of mind chatter like: *"What's the problem here?" "Why can't I hold still?"... etc.*

But the reality is, these tiny movements are your body's way of holding the pose (don't forget, you are on a rock hurtling through space after all) and are actually helping you get stronger!

These wiggles and wobbles of the poses (much like the challenges of life) are essential for you to develop the strength needed to stand your ground and stay centered on the mat AND off.

Rather than getting annoyed in these moments, learning to embrace them as opportunities to learn, grow, and evolve is key to you being able to handle the challenges of life that will inevitably come your way.

Consider this perspective shift next time you find yourself bobbing and weaving in a balance pose or when Zoom decides to update itself in the middle of your workshop and you're about to lose it. If this is happening for you, what is it teaching you?

That all being said, this shift is simple in theory but not always easy in practice. However, it will completely impact your ability to bounce back gracefully and continue forward on your journey equipped with new skills and knowledge.

So it's time to celebrate the YOU that you've become because of all that you've gone through by claiming out loud: **I am resilient**.

Now say it again. And then one more time a whole lot LOUDER this: **I AM RESILIENT!**

Because you are!

What does resilience mean to you?

Everything you've been through has helped you to learn and grow into who you are today. Consider some of your most challenging times: What have they taught you? What have they brought out of you?

Chapter Four

The Dark Cloud of Entrepreneurship

Have you ever woken up in the middle of the night with your heart pumping so hard it felt like you were about to cross the finish line of a race?

I'm talking full-on drenched in sweat, the sound of your heart pounding in your ears, and your mind instantly launching into every mistake you've ever made or the old stand-by:

"What the hell are you even doing trying to run a business? You have no freaking clue what you're doing."

(Spoiler alert: Most people don't.)

Then it instantly flashes your bank balance and credit card statements across the screen of the mental movie in your mind and then barks something to the effect of:

"So...yeah. There are still only pennies in your account, and your debt is growing by the day. What the heck are you gonna do?"

And then just for fun maybe adds: *"Who do you even think you're kidding with all this Business Owner nonsense? You should get a J.O.B.! This is never gonna work"*

It's kind of amazing, isn't it? How in the middle of the day, when you're supposed to be getting things done and creating content, writing emails, or something equally as important, and your brain is quieter than a mouse?

Then somewhere around 2 am or better yet, sixty minutes before your alarm goes off, it launches into full steam ahead, can't shut it up for the life of you mode.

One of those strange ironies of life I suppose. Or perhaps it's slightly more run-of-the-mill for us entrepreneurs.

The thing is, there's a dark side of entrepreneurship that not many people talk about.

While we are highly celebrated for our zest for life, enthusiasm, creativity, and general awesomeness, this intensity also has a built-in balancing mechanism. After all, the higher the highs, the lower the lows....

It likely will not surprise you that research from the University of California found that approximately 72% of entrepreneurs are challenged by ADD, ADHD, anxiety, depression, bipolar, or some combination of these. I share this with you not to scare you, but to remind you that if it is part of your reality too—you are definitely not alone. Many of us, myself included, are very much in that same boat with you.

I bring this up to give a voice to what I call: **The Dark Cloud of Entrepreneurship**. The invisible battles that we can come up against when blazing a trail in the world of business ownership.

Running your own business often means that you are the wearer of many hats. Learning to do many different things, often well out of your scope of expertise while trying to make it all work can definitely take a toll on you.

So is it any wonder your brain likes to wake you up in the middle of the night to remind you that you never replied to that email from your client? Or how you failed to come up with a clever reply to that troll on Instagram? Nope, not really.

It's one heck of a wild ride on the craziest non stop rollercoaster to be living and following your passion. It is certainly NOT easy to keep putting yourself out there and constantly questioning yourself as you do your best to figure it all out.

Is it any wonder our brains are all over the place? I don't think so.

To be honest, I do think it takes a special kind of person to be an entrepreneur. I mean, not everyone is willing to leap wildly into the unknown and figure out how to fly on the way down. You're a brave soul!

So what can you do when you're right about to launch another product, figure out a new software, or get on a sales call and the anxious racing of your heart makes you feel like a kite caught in a tornado?

What about when you wake up to your brain screaming: *"GO GO GO GO GO you have to get up and get GOING NOW!!!"*?

This can easily catapult you into a spiral of overwhelm leaving you wondering where the heck to even start since there's so much to do.

The answer is simple, but definitely not easy. Practice anchoring your mind to the point of focus so that you become centered and grounded.

Thankfully, Yoga has many incredible tools to help you do this. Through the poses, you can fully activate the power of physically grounding yourself into the mat. By tuning into your senses, you can ground yourself into your awareness of the NOW.

But perhaps the most powerful tool to ground yourself is your breath. In particular, shifting to a long and steady exhalation is so soothing to your nervous system that you'll likely notice a shift within just a few deep breaths.

Wanna try?

Sit up tall and relax your shoulders, jaw, and face.

Close your eyes and take a deep breath in through your nose to fill up your belly.

Keep inhaling until you feel full and then sip in a tiny bit more air.

Then exhale slowly through your mouth as you relax your face and neck and let it out with a big long slow HAAAAAAAAA sound. As you do this, focus on the feeling of becoming very relaxed and present.

Repeat this at least five more times and as you exhale mentally repeat to yourself: I AM GROUNDED as you feel yourself getting more settled with each breath.

Repeat as needed until you feel calm, centered, and ready to decide what your next step forward is.

Breathing. So simple but yet, so powerful...

Deep slow diaphragmatic breathing is so soothing to your nervous system that it is considered the #1 tool for reducing stress by the American Institute of Stress. This is because it has a very direct effect on your parasympathetic nervous system to shift you out of stress FAST!

Slowing down your breath helps to tone your vagus nerve, slows your heart rate, lowers your blood pressure, and shifts you into a grounded presence which of course are all wonderful things for you.

Lowering your stress is always a top priority considering it is not exactly the best for your health so it should be definitely a daily practice, especially when flying through life on the wings of a business.

Want some more fun facts about breathing? If you pay attention to them, your in and out breaths have very different qualities to them. As it fills you up and expands your lungs, your inhale is very invigorating and uplifting.

As you exhale, and your abdominals draw in to expel the breath out of your body it's very centering, helping you to get steady and anchored.

This means you can use the natural properties of the breath to your advantage. If you're wound up in a frantic frenzy about something, focus on doing a long slow exhale to ground you. Conversely, if you're feeling down and uninspired, allow your inhale to lift and open you up. Cool, right? I think so!!

Side note: In our ongoing search for the next best strategy or hack, we can easily lose sight of the ones right under our noses. Don't underestimate the power of a few deep breaths to help you come back to yourself! What the Yogis have known for thousands of years, modern science is repeatedly validating: the breath is a powerful tool.

So after you've taken deep breaths and are feeling like YOU again what do you do next?

Put your hands on your heart and connect to your Purposeful Powerhouse Higher Self and ask them what they would do. Keep breathing and feel for an answer. Maybe a name or an image will pop into your head, or maybe not.

Consulting with the wisdom of your heart is always a good idea and here's the good news: You certainly don't have to have it ALL figured out, you just need to decide on your next step forward.

Just like Virabhadra carving his way through the underground, little by little you're making your way there. But it all starts from consciously quieting the noisy chatter of your mind, coming back to your center, and listening for the quiet guidance of your heart.

So let's try that, shall we? Place your hands on the center of your chest, the seat of your emotional heart and breathe deeply. Let your exhale pass slowly out of your mouth as you mentally repeat: **I am grounded**.

Would you consider yourself a grounded person? If so, why? If not, is it something you'd like to become more of?

What helps you to feel grounded? How often do you do that?

Chapter Five

Meet Your Shitty Committee

"I came for the Yoga Booty and stayed for the inner peace."
~~~Megan Nolan~~~

It's true, I did. Admittedly, my first leap into the vast ocean that is Yoga was at my local gym. Since I've always loved exercise, I really enjoyed the physical challenge of the practice. And while I could hold the poses in my body, keeping my mind still was a WHOLE other story.

I literally could not get it to focus for more than 2 nanoseconds. Which to be honest, frustrated the heck out of me. Now, after years of teaching Yoga, I've come to realize that I'm certainly not the only one who feels this way.

In conversations with many other highly energetic, driven people, it's common for them to express the same sentiment. Many say that it was like their mind was trying to talk them out of doing the practice by saying it was boring, too slow, or that it was just not challenging enough for them.
~~~

Yoga is not for everyone. But what I do know is that while it means well, your mind is highly adept at talking you out of the very things that will help you learn and grow the most. After all, its main focus isn't about you expanding into your next level; it's far more interested in keeping you exactly where you are.

This is why anytime you're on the verge of doing something that will stretch you (literally and figuratively) your shitty committee goes into overdrive.

The shitty committee? Yep, you read that right. While you may not have ever heard it called that before, I'm guessing that you know EXACTLY what I'm talking about.

The voice in your head that talks shit. The one that makes you feel like crap. You know, the same one that doesn't do much other than the aforementioned tasks.

Hence the name.....

Maybe you call it the mean girl/guy/person, the inner critic, the victim mentality loop....whatever. We've all got them. The self-sabotaging characters in your head keeping you exactly where your brain thinks you should always be: safe, in your comfort zone.

While your brain is nothing short of a supercomputer, its main job is a very important one—to keep you alive.

Keenly focused on that, it has developed some ways of making sure you stay firmly planted in your zone of familiarity: The characters of your shitty committee AKA your self-sabotaging tendencies known as your Saboteurs.

The thing is, your mind is not interested in you going out on a limb and trying new things. It does not give one little damn about you expanding your consciousness and realizing how innately AH-mazing and powerful you are. Not even one.

The reality is, pretty much every task that's required of an entrepreneur falls into the category of **"Danger Zone"** from your brain's perspective.

Consider the following tasks (some of which might be old hat to you) that are actually really brave:

- Pressing that little red button to go live on Facebook and share your message with your community...

- Pouring your magic and wisdom into a new program and sharing it with the world...

- Sharing your personal stories and baring your soul in a book...

These are all courageous things that not many people are willing to do. But you are!

So is it any wonder that instead of writing the last chapter of your book, your brain is constantly suggesting that you clean out the junk drawer (again) instead of opening your laptop?

Or what about how it happily encourages you to change the font on your new PDF one more time before it's ready to share with your email list? Not surprising at all.

The very sneaky ways of procrastination, perfectionism, controlling, over-questioning, doomsday-ing and all the other stall tactics your brain uses are its way of keeping you exactly where you are right now.

So when it gets even the tiniest hint of you expanding yourself, (whether mentally, physically, or emotionally) it pulls out all the stops and rallies your self-sabotaging characters that may look and sound like this:

The Judge: Always the first to arrive on the scene and quickly find fault with you, anyone involved, or the situation. As the master Saboteur, the Judge then quickly recruits any of the following characters to trip you up.

The Hyper Achiever: Pushing you to do more, work harder, saying you're not doing enough and promising you'll be happy when you've achieved your goals (and no sooner).

The Stickler: Perfectionistic tendencies that leave you on a constant journey of making it better or perfect by setting insanely high standards for yourself and others

The Avoider: Instead of taking action or having the difficult conversation you'll doing anything else, the whole time beating yourself up for not doing it and feeling totally stressed about it.

The Victim: The slippery slope of believing that nothing ever works out for you or that life is extremely rigged against you. This leaves you feeling discouraged and frozen in doubt.

The Restless: The ultimate Shiny Squirrel Syndrome that has you hopping all over the place in search of the next best thing or wanting to be able to do it all so you don't miss out on anything.

The Hyper Vigilant: Focusing on the worst-case scenario or in a constant state of worry or stress like the "Boy Who Cried Wolf" which can leave you exhausted mentally or physically.

The Controller: Taking responsibility for everything yourself and being unwilling to delegate it out to others out of fear it won't be done to your standards which often results in overworking or resentment.

The Pleaser: Always seeking love, approval, and acceptance this Saboteur will have you struggling to set boundaries or say "*No*" to requests because you want to help others. Although it's with good intentions, it can also lead to you feeling resentful and frustrated when your needs are not met, or you feel taken advantage of.

The Hyper Rational: Convincing you that decisions are best made without emotion, this Saboteur can cause others to see you as cynical or cold which can leave you feeling misunderstood and alienated.

Any of those sound vaguely familiar? I figured so. Whether yours sound just like that or have a slightly different tone, they all have one thing in common: *they end up making you feel like POOP.*

The Saboteurs in your head attempt to motivate you through negative emotions and usually end up causing you all sorts of negative emotions like sadness, shame, disappointment, regret, resentment, or jealousy.

They force you into the "Happy When" syndrome: the trap of believing that ONLY once you've got 10K followers, have an international bestseller, or are earning $100K/ year you'll FINALLY be good enough, happy, successful, or worthy.

Here's the plot twist....

Most of the time, even when you achieve those things or your version of them, the feeling of achievement is fleeting and empty because the Saboteurs soon show up and try to sell you on the next best thing.

That is, if they even let you celebrate it at all because they'll likely have a few snide remarks to say about how it all went. They literally will find fault and issues with everything, everyone, and _especially you._ If you let them.

Do you see the painful irony here? The shitty committee in your head will run the show if you let it AND make you feel crappy in the process.

Which is exactly what was happening to my student Tricia. Each morning she woke up with heart-pounding anxiety and spent the day feeling like she was on a speeding train of stress she couldn't get off. She was at her wit's end when she first came to me asking if Yoga could help her feel like herself again.

Thankfully, the tools of the practice helped her to feel calm, grounded, and realize what was happening in her brain to make her feel that way.

Now she knows exactly what to do when she catches the captain of her committee (who she calls Restless Rodney) up to his old antics and causing her to bounce all over the place with worry.

She pauses, gets grounded by using the tools she's learned in Yoga, and then from that place of awareness decides what to do next. This means she's able to stay focused and get more done in less time, plus have time and energy left over to enjoy her life at the end of the day.

Can you now see why Yoga is so focused on taking back control from the mind? Because unless you learn to command it, it will run you. Hopefully, it's a little more clear now why I included the story of Virabhadra in this book to give you an ancient toolset that is applicable in your modern entrepreneurial life!

So how do you take back the reins from your Saboteurs? It starts with one very simple yet innately complex tool: awareness.

You begin to pay attention to your mind and its oh-so sneaky ways. By noticing your habits, reactions, and patterns, you'll begin to see how you react to life when it gets challenging.

It all starts with observation. Being willing to slow down enough to pay attention to the noisy chatter in your head is no easy feat. But WOW is it an eye-opening experience.

Wondering where these habits come from? Childhood.

Typically created before the age of 6 when your brain is still forming, these patterns were formed without your conscious knowledge since that part of your brain, your prefrontal cortex, wasn't formed yet. You developed habits by modeling the ones happening around you so that you would continue to be loved and cared for in your tribe, community, or family of origin. Interesting, right?

While they are hard-wired into your brain, you can actually shift them, by first becoming aware of them. Since your brain is changeable (thank the heavens!!), you can create new ones by thinking new thoughts and choosing different responses. In doing so, you are essentially updating your inner operating system of beliefs to align with who you are today!

Think of how many times you've updated your phone or computer's operating system. Probably a few, right? YOUR inner operating system needs the same upgrade otherwise it too will be getting glitchy and causing all sorts of problems.

Be warned though, catching the Saboteur shitty committee in action is like trying to catch your shadow. It will shapeshift and change tactics to continue to do its job: keep you right where you are: safe and sound.

But as soon as you start to shine the light of your awareness on them, they cannot be unseen. So you can begin to notice them, pause to ground yourself, and then from the place of connection and presence decide on what to do next.

This is true power: learning to think and act on purpose to move you closer towards your mission, just like your Warrior guide Virabhadra. Think about how much awareness you get to practice in Warrior One pose!

By pressing through your feet, you get to cultivate a deep connection to the mat and a steady activation of your leg muscles. As you keep your breath smooth and deep, you activate your core to lengthen your spine up as you reach your arms to the ceiling.

Internally, you are constantly scanning for where you can soften and let go of tension as you engage in other parts of your body you are fine-tuning your focus. All the while, the deeper work of the pose is to find that sweet spot where your mind, body, and spirit all intersect in union and stillness. Talk about an exercise in awareness!

So are you willing to become a witness to your mind and its sneaky self-sabotaging ways so you can learn to keep your attention on your intention to bring your big vision to life? I hope so!

Take a deep breath in and declare it with me: **I Am Aware!** If you're ready to continue the journey forward.

    **A note on the Saboteurs! These sneaky little buggers were discovered by Shirzad

Chamine and are an integral part of the Positive Intelligence® framework that has transformed my life. Please see the link in bio to learn more.

What do the characters of your shitty committee sound like?

How do they show up in your life? How do they make you feel?

Ready to fully experience a deeply grounded awareness and activate these essential tools? Experience for yourself how Yoga does that.

Scan QR code or go to https://bit.ly/TWJBsection1 to be guided through a transformative Yoga practice and discover which pose is best for your personality type!

SECTION TWO: VIRABHADRA ARRIVES…

After much determination and focus, Virabhadra has now finally made his way to the party. *Keep in mind, inside the palace is already quite the scene:* Daksha and the guests are devastated and grief-stricken as they stand in shock around Sati's ashes.

Then, without warning, Virabhadra pierces a hole through the floor of the palace and explodes into the center of the party. What a sight for them to see: a wild being with a thousand heads and thousand arms each one carrying a sword—kind of scary, I'm sure!

The guests, terrified, pull back in fear as he strikes a power pose (Warrior Two) and with all eyes on him, yells loudly: *"Who is Daksha? My master sends for you!"*

With nowhere to hide and knowing exactly who sent this vicious Warrior, Daksha steps forward timidly and whispers: *"I am Daksha"*.

Virabhadra locks his gaze on him, and all the guests freeze in terror as they wait to see what will happen.

In this moment, Virabhadra is the epitome of strength and steadiness. Fully owning his presence and power, deeply connected to the truth of who he is, our Warrior commands the attention of the entire room.

What a potent gift and skill right? Clearly, one that is useful for you too in the moments when you get to dig in, stand your ground and be present as you own your powerful place in the spotlight as a visionary, thought leader, and inspiring entrepreneur.

Let's explore the tools in depth...

Chapter Six

Finding Your Stick

Entrepreneurship: The lesson in personal development you didn't know you needed.

Hot damn. If I had any idea what was ahead for me when I entered the wild world of business ownership, I'm not sure if I would have been full steam ahead with it.

"Open a business, it will be great to be your own boss," they say...

"Work for yourself, you get to make your own hours," they say...

Nobody tells you about the thousand hats you'll get to wear, all the things you'll get to learn (and hopefully, one day, master), and how vulnerable it is to constantly be putting yourself out in the world.

The struggle is real. But so is the growth. And if you're honest, would you really have it any other way?

But the truth is: half the battle in growing your business is staying focused on your vision. Keeping your eye on the prize as the saying goes.

Isn't Virabhadra a fantastic example of this? He focused on his target until he got there. Had he not, he likely would have ended up crashing some other unsuspecting party, nowhere near the target.

That being said, given that many entrepreneurs are multi-passionate and typically have many projects on the go simultaneously, this is NO easy feat!

Reining your mind is often quite the challenge for many of us, and then throw in the stress, caffeine, excitement, and sleep deprivation, and you're in a whole other league of difficulty.

Ask it to hold still, and your mind literally wants to be everywhere. Usually anywhere *but* the place you want it to be.

It makes sense though, since it's the nature of your mind to be busy. Averaging anywhere between 60,000-70,000 thoughts a day, there's a lot going on in that sweet noggin of yours.

Mine too, which is why I avoided meditation for the longest time. I did at least give it *"the old college try"* (as my Mum calls it), but admittedly, it wasn't long before I quit.

Why? Because it was H A R D. I could not for the life of me get my brain to settle down. This elusive inner peace that meditation was meant to help me experience was replaced by a whole lot of worrying, wondering, and wandering all over the place.

I got annoyed, and frustrated, and eventually gave up.

Then my would Saboteurs kick in, taunting me with thoughts like:

"Some kind of Yoga teacher you are...you don't even meditate."

"Can you really even say you're practicing Yoga without meditating? Don't think so."

This would temporarily spur me into action as I really value integrity and practicing what I preach.

So I'd try again, only to give up shortly after completely irritated by the incessant chattering monkey collective in my skull and promising to start again next week.

But I didn't.

That is until my Grandmother was diagnosed with Alzheimer's. This freaked me out for her, my Grandfather, my Mum and aunts, my siblings, and me.

So out of curiosity and concern, I started researching the best things you can do to keep your brain healthy and hopefully prevent such diseases.

Wanna know one of the most powerful things you can do to protect your brain from accelerated age-related decline (in addition to a well-balanced diet, cardiovascular exercise, and lowering stress)?

Yep. You guessed it: Meditate

While cardiovascular exercise encourages your brain to grow new neurons (aka, your brain cells), meditation helps them to mature. It turns out that the challenge of constantly returning your mind to the point of focus is actually what makes it so good for you.

Who knew? Apparently, the Yogis were onto something ....*again*. Such smart cookies they are.

So, re-inspired about my meditation practice I went to my teacher Nicki Doane to ask for her advice on meditation. When I shared my cerebral dilemma with her, she gave me a classically intriguing Yoga teacher-type answer:

"Well, maybe you haven't found your stick yet..."

Nope. I certainly had not found my stick.

I pondered this for a second, wondering if I had missed a very important lesson during my Yoga Teacher Training, then asked: *"Could you explain that to me, please? I didn't know I needed a stick to meditate..."*

She laughed and began:

"Your mind is like an elephant. It's wise and curious, always picking things up and dropping them. Wandering to and fro aimlessly, UNLESS it's given something to do.

Something to hold on to.

This is why often when you see elephants holding a stick or another elephant's tail. Their handlers give them that to hold so they stay on track and reach their destination without too much distraction."

I pondered this for a moment and asked:

"So, my mind is the elephant? And the stick is something for it to do or focus on to keep it steady and focused?"

"Exactly" she replied and continued: *"You need to find your stick,"* and laughed with a smile and a wise twinkle in her eye.

So off I went to find my stick. I searched high and low in the forest of tools and realized she was right: <u>*I had not found my stick.*</u>

Sitting and observing my breath clearly had not worked for me.

Being so used to doing a million different things at once and leapfrogging all over the place meant that when asked to be still, my mind would instantly rebel.

"Hahahaha, just try to quiet me" it would taunt. And then launch into full chattering monkey mode—definitely not peacefully whatsoever!

So the quest began. You know what the first thing I realized was? There are a whole freaking lot of ways to meditate. Laughing, walking, silent, chanting, painting, I mean you name it, and there's probably someone teaching how to meditate that way.

The beauty is, they're all taking you toward the same goal: *presence*.

Each one of these modes of meditation, if practiced diligently will help you anchor your mind to the point of focus so you can slow it down and hopefully experience a glimpse of sweet stillness.

A chance to float on the ocean of calm in between the waves of thought and just be....

Lingering there for as long as possible until you realize you've dropped the stick (ie: got distracted in thought), pick it back up, and begin again.

Let me tell you, when you get to that space, (even if just for a millisecond) ***it is magical!*** Time slows to a halt, and the connection to yourself and the universe is profound. The experience is absolutely delicious.

Then just like that: WHOOSHHHHH you're off thinking about launch funnels and email copy.

Or pondering the great mysteries of life, like how junk manages to get on the ceiling or why you can't seem to find your favorite pair of socks.....I mean seriously important quandaries. It happens.....a lot.

Actually, it turns out that getting distracted, noticing that, and then returning to your point of attention is actually why meditation is so beneficial for your brain. Called *"effortful learning"*, this situation explains that because keeping your mind on task is SO challenging, it is exactly what encourages your neurons to mature and strengthen.

So every time you recognize that you've drifted off in thought and then return to your point of focus, it strengthens the part of your brain responsible for this called the hippocampus. This is relevant because this is the part of the brain potentially affected by the changes that can happen with age, as well as when people experience depression. So the more you can do to keep it healthy, the better!

By helping you to maintain your memory and elevate your mood meditation sure is MAGICAL, isn't it?!

Then you throw in the other benefits like:

>lowering your stress levels so you don't feel like living life on a high-speed train that never slows down let alone stops

>helping you sleep better so you actually wake up refreshed and ready for the day

>boosting immune function so you get sick less often and recover faster when you do

>developing command of your mind so you can learn to think on purpose and use your mind as the powerful tool it is

>increasing your patience so you don't lose your shit at people constantly

>and generally making you a more calm, happy, and nicer person to be around

Considering all of that, is it any wonder why the Yogis made it the goal of the entire Yoga practice? I don't think so.

Kinda makes you want to go find your stick, doesn't it?

Keep in mind though it may take a few tries to figure out which one(s) work for you.

Interestingly, this is also a useful lesson in entrepreneurship. For many business owners, it often takes a while for you to find your niche, refine your message, figure out what the heck you're doing, and actually get traction in your business.

It's a whole damn lot of dropping the stick, picking it up, and coming back to the moment at hand. Finding your focus and beginning again.

Moral of the story: Stay open and keep going. With your meditation practice, with your business, your niche, how you like to exercise, whatever.....*maybe you just haven't found your stick yet.*

This was the case for my client Amber...until we began working together. As a busy lady with lots on the go, she admitted to me that self-care felt like something she had to add to her already mile-long to-do list. When I asked why that was, she said she had fallen out of love with exercise.

"Let's change that," I said. *"How do you LIKE to exercise?"*

"I love to dance," she replied excitedly. *"And I love knowing why I'm doing things so I really GET it. It helps me understand why it's helpful so I want to actually do it."*

Off we went! Every session we did together included dance breaks and awesome tunes (SO FUN!!). As we did the exercises and poses, I explained what they were helping her activate and strengthen so she could experience them in a totally new way. Which often led to her proclaiming: *"WOW!! So that's what they're supposed to feel like. I totally get it now!"*

After working together, she released over 60 pounds and is happily living from a space of ease and flow. Plus, she's fallen in love with Yoga and exercise again!!

Pretty AH-mazing what can happen when you find your flow with things, right?

So, put your hand on your heart and pause. Acknowledge how far you've come and get present to your OWN radiant presence and just breathe.

Witness yourself for a second. Not many people have it in them to do what you do. Nor can they do it like you do.

Breathe that in and just ***Be Present***. Be a witness to all that you've brought to life and all that you are.

Whisper (or heck yell it out if you want): ***"I Am Present"*** as you practice the beautiful (but not so easy) art of just BE-ing Here Now!

Take a moment to reflect on everything you've been through as an entrepreneur. You've been through a lot, learned many lessons, and grown into the YOU you are today.

Write a letter to the past version of you who is about to start your business. Tell them what is to come and who you are now because of it.

Chapter Seven

Down The Waterslide

"You're FAR more powerful than you give yourself credit for." ~~~Me~~~

Ironically, but not surprisingly I coined this beautiful quote at a time when I was feeling lost, frustrated, and truly quite discouraged....again. I had just wrapped up a long promotional period to invite people into one of my programs.

The goal was to welcome 25 people into the group, but instead, I welcomed NONE. Not for lack of trying mind you, I went all out. After weeks of promo to a free workshop series, I taught my heart out during that live event. And when I opened the doors, no one signed up.

While I was hoping for the pinging sound of notifications about new community members, all I heard were crickets.

Well, that, and the noisy barrage of judgemental commentary happening inside my head. My Saboteurs were having a HEYDAY.

The best way I can describe the experience was kind of like being pushed down a waterslide head first.

Imagine this:

Me standing innocently at the top of the waterslide when my Judgey Inner Critic trips me up and pushes me onto the slide by critiquing everything I did in the workshop.

All the places I screwed up and went wrong go flashing before my eyes as the downward spiral of self-doubt begins...

Next, my Hyper Achiever starts greasing the slide with the very familiar feeling of failure because I came nowhere near my goal. Berating me with disappointment and feelings of emptiness.

Then my Hyper Vigilant Saboteur pipes up and starts hosing the slide down with money worries and the sinking reminder of my growing debt, and I felt myself tunneling head first totally out of control.

Finally, after the twists and turns, I flew into the impending pool of sadness and disappointment only to be held under the water by my Victim's moanings of why the hell things always go like this for me.

I cough and sputter for a while, eventually making my way up for air. Feeling very defeated and discouraged.

I told you those buggers are nasty. Perhaps you've had a similar experience with yours? The negative shitstorm in the head is REAL.

In those moments, my Yoga mat was always my solace, giving me the space to float to the surface and just rest.

In that quiet stillness, I finally realized how much torment my mind was actually causing me. The amount of pain I was allowing it to inflict was actually quite shocking. But as you remember, of the many jobs your brain has, its number one task is your survival.

While what I was doing in my launch wasn't really life-threatening, it was scary AF to my brain. I was doing things that stretched me, made me vulnerable, and showcased me in a way that might cause me to be rejected.

So it did what it was meant to do. Kept me right where I was. In my comfort zone, safe and sound.

The truth is, it had reason to be concerned. Not just because I might get laughed at, but because in the span of my many lives, there was a time when I was violently persecuted for my gifts.

Putting aside your own views on the afterlife for a second, the law of conservation of energy states that energy can neither be created nor destroyed. It can merely change forms.

So this means that each of us has changed forms an unlimited number of times, whether in this life or in others. And it turns out, in one of my previous lives I was killed for being a high priestess of magic and healing.

This means that this memory was stored in my DNA, giving my brain a completely justifiable reason to vigilantly protect me from doing anything that really showcased my gifts.

That came out of left field didn't it? You're telling me. I mean, I've always known I was magical but holy moly, discovering I was burnt at the stake was quite the revelation.

How I discovered this part of me is a WHOLE other story, but let me tell you it was an intense journey into the depths of my psyche. Luckily, I had support and guidance in navigating the experience, hypnotherapy on multiple occasions to shift and heal it, and I'm far more powerful for having experienced all of it.

So after I put the pieces together and figured out why my Saboteurs reacted so strongly to me putting myself in the world, everything made a whole lot more sense.

Understandably, due to the fact that I had been killed in a past life for being myself, I get why my brain was pulling out all the stops. It perceived what I was doing as HIGHLY DANGEROUS.

Side Note: The thing about these subconscious reactions is that they're buried deep in your mind in a storehouse of memories. Your mind is constantly scanning your surroundings and comparing everything to past experiences and then using that information to influence your reaction. As brilliant as it is, your brain has no reference to time and treats every bit of information it uncovers as though it's happening NOW.

Hence the reason you react so strongly in situations that trigger memories of the past that impacted you. It instantly takes you back to that moment in time whether that was back to reading a speech in front of your grade six class in this current timeline or leading a Winter Solstice ceremony in the ancient fields of Scotland in a past life. Pretty wild, right?

Thankfully, as you learned earlier you can actually rewire your brain and create a new reality for yourself. Although the operating system was installed many years ago, you can begin to shift your beliefs and ways of being by intentionally choosing new thoughts and responses in any situation.

Since your brain has no sense of what you're imagining with vivid detail and what's REALLY happening you can completely use this to your advantage in a few ways:

- by focusing on your goals you allow your mind the opportunity to mentally rehearse what they will look and feel like to give it a sense of famil-iarity and safety with them

- re-imagining a situation that didn't go as planned the way you wanted it to go instead. Doing so actually causes new neural pathways to be developed and makes it more likely you'll respond that way in the future.

Keep in mind, this can also work against you! By men-tally reliving and beating yourself for a mistake over and over you strengthen that neural pathway and make it more likely that you'll repeat that same frustrating pattern again. Yep. Self-sabotage at its finest.

When you consider that, is it any wonder that you see patterns happening repeatedly in your life? It's literally hardwired into your brain until you do the work of updating the program you're running.

Pretty incredible, right?

So what does this mean for you? **Firstly:** Stop going back and beating yourself up for your mistakes!! It's a waste of your precious time and energy.

Instead, go back and ask yourself how your higher self would have handled the situation. Visualize yourself taking that action. Then repeat. Over and over!

Fun fact: This is the mechanics behind why visualization is so impactful.

Visualizing a situation gives your brain an experience of you achieving your goal. By seeing it in your mind's eye you're also making it more safe and familiar, so that it becomes perceivable and less threatening. Isn't your brain cool?

As you may have guessed, visualization was a huge part of the healing of my past life experience. Re-visioning the ceremony by having the persecutors join us in the gathering and become part of our community allowed me to create safety in my system and shift my memory of it.

I also use the re-visioning technique after the many times I've gone headfirst down the metaphorical waterslide of self-sabotage. Once I catch it happening, I pause and become present, then see myself vigilantly watching for the Saboteurs tactics, taking command of my mind, and coming back to the energy of my vision.

Sometimes I'm able to catch myself before it happens and other times I'm well into the deep end of self-doubt and inner nastiness before I even realize what's happened. Then I climb back out and begin again. Thankfully, with practice, I'm now able to catch things sooner and recover much faster.

The key is to not allow your brain to judge any part of the process. After all, it's really a practice in learning to do the most challenging thing of all: *control your own mind.*

But when you do, wow is it POWERFUL. Learning to think on purpose is hands down of the most effective tools you need to achieve your goals!

The truth is, you already have the capability to do it. You simply need to cultivate it. Practice it again and again.

So my incredible wise Warrior reader, let's claim it here and now by commanding your mind to focus on your breath. Breathe slowly and deeply and vigilantly watch for hard your mind works to try to take you anywhere but the present moment.

Repeat for at least 10 slow deep belly breaths as you mentally repeat **I Am Powerful** with every exhale.

Remember, getting your mind to stay focused is very much like training a puppy to *"Sit and Stay."* First, you give it the command, then continually go and check on it. Sometimes it will be exactly where you left it, and other times it will have wandered off getting into trouble somewhere. Patiently keep trying, and eventually, you'll be able to get it to hold steady. The key is persistence, it is a practice after all.

Repeat **I Am Powerful** one more time and then check in with yourself. Notice your inner power rising up in celebration of you acknowledging it! You are a powerful being, my friend. Celebrate that; own that!

"Between the stimulus and the response, there is a pause. That pause is your place of power." Viktor Frankl

How often do you pause throughout the day to check in with yourself and return to your center?

When do you feel the most powerful? What helps you experience that? Do you do that intentionally?

Want to fully awaken the full potential of the present moment and tap into your own boundless possibility?

Scan QR code or go to https://bit.ly/TWJBsection2 to take a Power Pause Yoga practice. Plus learn which balancing breathwork technique to use based on your specific personality type!

SECTION THREE: MISSION ACCOMPLISHED

Let's return once more to the scene inside the party...

The guests are still reeling from Sati's death and now standing before them in the middle of the room is Virabhadra: a ferocious-looking Warrior with a thousand heads and arms, each one carrying a sword.

Sent by a furious Shiva to avenge Sati's death, Virabhadra now stands before Daksha who is trembling in fear knowing exactly what is about to happen.

Virabhadra's voice booms out again: *"My Master Shiva sends for you,"* as he gracefully steps towards him and in one quick swipe of his sword lops off Daksha's head.

Being so deeply bonded to her father, Sati instantly regains her physical form and calls out to Shiva: *"SHIVA! I know you're behind this! Fix this NOW"*.

Instantly knowing he overreacted and made a terrible mistake, Shiva transports himself to the party within seconds. Grateful to see Sati alive, but sheepishly aware of his error, Shiva grabs the most suitable head he can find (one from a goat on the buffet table) and places it on Daksha's body.

Drawing a deep breath in, he exhales life back into Daksha. Grateful to be alive once again, Daksha apologizes for his behavior and decides to turn the party into a celebration of Shiva and Sati's love!

See?! I told you it was a crazy story! I hope it's now more obvious to you why I included this ancient tale of a courageous and determined Warrior on a mission.

The path forward on your mission will be filled with many unpredictable twists and turns, however, each one of them has so much to teach you.

As it was for Virabhadra, there will be times that require you to blaze your own trail and others that ask you to stand in your strength and truly own who you are. Many of these will culminate in moments that invite you to dig deep and be relentless in the pursuit of your dreams and goals.

Now, let's dive into what this final chapter of Virabhadra's story has to teach you about being committed to charging forward bravely on your soul's mission and what it will *really* take for you to bring your vision to life.

Chapter Eight

It's Not As Scary As It Sounds

It takes an incredible level of commitment to make your way through the twists and turns of launching and running a business. Not to mention constantly stepping forward into the spotlight and taking brave action towards your goals as Virabhadra did. I am SO freaking proud of you!

To be honest with you, I think entrepreneurs are a special kind of crazy (said with the utmost love and respect). I mean who else is willing to keep showing up and going after it the way you do?

It is NOT EASY.

There have been many times when I have described being an entrepreneur as running toward a giant wall and attempting to leap over it. More times than I can count it has felt like I ran straight into it and was thrown right back down on my butt.

Humbled. Discouraged. Frustrated. Confused.

Soon I learned that there are easier ways to get over the wall from others that have gone before me. Learning from coaches and others further along in their journey has been a saving grace.

Their guidance was like a rope being thrown down to help me with the climb. While these mentors offered the pathway, the effort to join them was still my own. Always being one to blaze my own trail, I would often take their advice and then try to create my own way which usually ended up with me right back where I started....on my butt staring back at the wall.

Eventually I heard something that one of my coaches, James Wedmore had been saying all along: *"Respectfully, until you've had a million-dollar launch, just follow the strategy and don't mess with it"*.

So I did. I haven't had a million-dollar launch (YET!!), but I followed the core of his advice: Commit. Pick a path and go with it.

Trust me, I resisted this for many many years and looking back, I realize how much it taught me. But also how much it cost me.

I was all over the place. Pivoting left and right. I spent so much time and energy constantly starting over. Trying this new strategy, that new funnel....always looking for the missing piece.

It's all part of the process of course, but I share this in hopes of saving you a few meltdowns and smackdowns of your own.

Whatever you choose to focus on, *go all in on it.* Make the vision of what you have for your life and business expansive, bold, and inspirational!

Connect to the future version of you that has achieved these goals and explore what accomplishing them makes possible for you, your family, the people you get to support, and your community, go as big and wide as you can imagine. In doing so, you make the goals BIGGER than you!

Let's try something fun! Ask yourself the following questions:

How does that future you that has already achieved your goals stand and carry themselves?

How do they start their day? What does their inner dialogue sound like?

This is all essential information in helping you live into that vision today and bring it to life with more ease and speed

What does the energy of your vision feel like to you? What emotions does that future version of you experience every day as they live in that reality?

I call these your *"North Star"* emotions because they are so powerful! They become a guiding light in the sky that will help you to navigate toward that vision with ease and speed.

You've likely heard tapping into your future self energy and emotions explained before as: *"acting as if"* or *"assuming the feeling of your wish fulfilled"* as Dr. Wayne Dyer called it, and it's all correct.

Here's why:

"Everything is energy, and that's all there is to it. Match the frequency of the reality you desire and it cannot help but be yours. This is not philosophy, this is physics." ~
~~Albert Einstein~~~

In speaking to the law of attraction and vibration, Einstein summed it up well and was essentially saying:

You are energy. Everything about you has a measurable frequency to it, including your emotions. By living in the feelings of your vision (ie: Your North Star emotions) you'll be a match to opportunities, people, and experiences that align with your goals and be open to receiving them into your life. Thus making them and your vision a reality more quickly.

While you also need to commit to showing up and doing the work of the nitty-gritty of running a business, I've realized that the true dedication required of you as an entrepreneur is:

Being so wholeheartedly dedicated to your vision that nothing will stop you from achieving it.

Because the truth is, (if it hasn't happened already), I can say from experience that it's very likely that at some point on your journey, that:

>Your voice will shake when you speak when your nerves are rumbling in your belly.

>A launch may have 0 sales, causing you to question the worth of your program and work.

>You'll create amazing content that no one will ever see....except maybe your #1 fans that thanks to the algorithm see everything you post.

>Workshops will be delivered to your dog when no one else joins you in the Zoom room. While he's cute and all he doesn't have any feedback or a credit card, so is definitely not your aligned right client.

>Your Saboteurs will scream so loud it will be nearly impossible to hear the quiet whispers of your heart telling you to get up and try again.

These things happen to all of us.

But as the saying goes: *"It's not about how many times you fall down. It's about how many times you get back up."* ~~~ *Jamie Escalante*~~~

Sometimes, you'll get up gracefully and quickly. Other times you won't, but it's all part of the process. It's a practice after all, and the more you do it, the stronger you get. Just like when you stand in a balance pose like Warrior Three. There is a whole lot going on all at once!

The commitment required to plant one foot as you lift the other one up and reach it back behind you is next level. Leaning forward from the hip you stretch your upper body forward like an arrow heading toward the target just like Virabhadra did.

Plus, there are so many factors at play such as your strength, flexibility, breath, awareness, and focus that all impact the pose. As your body adjusts to meet the challenges of gravity and balancing on one foot, your commitment will absolutely be tested.

Will you tumble out and try again? Or will you get frustrated and give up? Your call.

In truth, mastering any pose usually means tipping out of it many times over. Not only does this teach humility and give you a deeper understanding of its subtleties, but it also really strengthens your commitment to your practice and growth.

All of which have beautiful applications OFF the mat too! All of this non-judgemental self-awareness cultivated in your practice also helps you to:

- become quicker at catching yourself in the spirals of self-sabotage so you stop wasting your power on it

- get faster at finding the lessons and letting go of the rest to bounce back faster and stronger

- learn that beating yourself up for mistakes is a waste of your precious time, energy, and it really just makes you feel like crap anyways so what's the point?

By committing to witnessing your habits and patterns you'll learn to question your thoughts and soon begin to use your mind like the powerful tool that it is.

And.....if you haven't already, you'll remember that you are downright freaking AH-mazing.

Of course, this will all take a dedicated commitment to your vision and yourself. But in doing so you'll be that much closer to the ultimate reward: becoming the most vibrantly alive and joyful expression of YOU.

This is exactly what my client Erin was able to do! Given she loved her work as a soulful social media coach and strategist so much, she struggled to pull away from her business to do something for herself. However, all the long hours at her desk were causing all sorts of weird aches, pains, and stress which she really didn't like.

Working together, she realized that in order to bring her big vision to life, she needed to be vibrantly holistically healthy so she committed to that fully.

Weaving intention into our sessions allowed her to connect powerfully with her mind, body, and spirit so she can show up in full alignment in all areas of her life and business. Now, she makes her self-care a top priority and is fully committed to showing up for herself because of how it makes her feel! Fantastic, right?

So, are you in?

Then stand up tall, draw your shoulders back and hold yourself with confidence and say it LOUD and PROUD: **I Am Committed!**

Commitment can be a scary word for some people. Is that true for you? If so, how does that show up in your life and work?

If not, how do you feel being committed has impacted the path of your life and business? Is there such a thing as being too committed (ie: stuck in your ways and having trouble going with the flow)?

What are you ready to commit to in your life and business that you can take action on TODAY?

Chapter Nine
The Missing Piece

"If I asked you to name all the things you love, how long would it take for you to name yourself?"

The first time I read that question I was struck by a wave of overwhelming emotion when I realized that I wouldn't have made my own list.

wow.

It rattled me to my core and made me very sad when I saw how often I was withholding love from myself.

I witnessed for the first time how I was really treating myself and was so sad for the little girl inside of me that longed for and truly deserved deep unconditional love.

Of course, we hear about self-love all the freaking time: Why it's necessary, what it does for you, etc.

But what we don't hear enough about is how to **actually** love yourself.

Now let's pause for a second. While I'm all about you getting pedicures and massages, that is not what we're talking about here.

We're not talking about self-care. Although as a personal trainer, Yoga instructor, and mental fitness coach you know I'm all about you taking care of yourself on every level of your mind, body, and spirit.

But by true authentic self-love, I mean a deep appreciation for the magical being that is you. A full acceptance of all parts of you: the ones you're proud of, the ones that bother you, the ones you wish had never happened..... all of you.

Dimples, wrinkles, gray hairs, no hairs, every last little bit of you.

For many of us, this is not an easy task! Partly because no one really teaches you how to really do this, but mostly because of that nasty collective of shit-talking critics in your head that can make it really hard to do at times.

With a hard focus on faults, flaws, and mistakes your Saboteurs (and in particular your Judge) really want you to believe that you are not quite yet deserving of true approval and acceptance.

It can be a hard pill to swallow that your own brain is so focused on you being better, more, less, or different than you are before you deserve unconditional love.

This is especially true for those among us who are very hyper-achieving, controlling, perfectionistic, or all of those things combined.

These tendencies can cause you to set extremely high standards for yourself and when not achieved can often cause a backlash of self-deprecating talk and actions. Even when you achieve your goals, the celebration is usually fleeting (if it happens at all) before the next one is set and your focus is shifted from the win to what's next.

The truth is, this constant striving is like a hungry beast that is never satisfied. Being on a constant quest for more wins, achievements, certifications, and accolades to prove your worthiness, enoughness, and deservedness means the quest never stops.....that is until we realize that the approval we all want absolutely must come from within first.

So how do you truly cultivate this unconditional self-love and acceptance that has long been touted as the key for true and lasting happiness and success?

As you learned in chapter three, it all starts with awareness. Learning to witness your habits and patterns so you can then practice non-judgemental observation and consciously decide how to move forward. The key is that once you notice yourself in an old pattern NOT to allow your Judge to kick in and make you wrong for doing it in the first place.

On the mat: You're a couple of breaths into Warrior Two pose and you decide to check what your back arm is doing in the pose. Upon inspection, you notice that instead of being strongly stretched back it's just dangling there not up to much.

By practicing non-judgemental awareness you don't make it wrong, you just notice it and then change it. You take a breath, roll your shoulders back, and engage your arm muscles as you reach out through your fingers.

"When you know better, you do better," as Maya Angelou said.

This is what I told myself when I realized how I had been depriving myself of the love and approval that my soul deeply craved.

As many entrepreneurs do, I had a lifetime of priding myself as a hard worker under my belt when I realized that I was defining myself by my achievements and failures.

I was constantly pushing myself for more. Trying to get to the elusive "next level" with little to no appreciation for the effort I was putting into things or for the evolution that was happening along the way.

Yet, I was struggling to achieve my goals, and I was always wondering why they weren't happening. I mean, I was working hard, doing all the things, so what was the problem?

But the truth was, I was always working from a place of wanting to prove myself. Pushing harder and then collapsing under the weight of feeling like a failure, the self-critical spiral would quickly swallow me whole and pull me under again.

The ongoing critique was terribly harsh, but I told myself it was necessary to improve and get where I wanted to go. To be honest, I was horrible to myself mentally. Setting insanely high standards and goals and then pushing myself to get there, yet when I got nowhere close, I was deeply disappointed and discouraged.

Whatever the problem of the moment was became my obsession. I would quickly turn my frustration and disappointment back on myself and launch into the usual internal nastiness. It was brutal.

One day when I was in a crumpled heap and puddle of tears yet again, a vision of myself as a little girl flashed before my eyes.

I saw myself hiding in the corner of a room sobbing and rocking back and forth. I looked so small and fragile that I was overcome with a deep tenderness towards her that I so badly wanted to hold and console her.

As she lifted her weary eyes to look at me I realized exactly what was happening. She so desperately wanted to be seen, held and loved exactly as she was. Not for what she had done, but simply because she was.

At that moment, it became so clear to me what was happening in my life:

Rather than celebrating the lessons and growth I was withholding love and encouragement from myself in the very moments when I needed it the most.

Which would cause me to shrink back with disappointment and sadness, again and again.

My heart was craving love and approval but all I was giving myself was the exact opposite. Which of course left me feeling unseen, broken, and empty.

The vicious cycle would continue, that is until I chose to use my newfound awareness and a very powerful tool to change it.

The tool that I used to begin to fall in love with myself might surprise you. It was a picture of me as a child. So young and vibrant, with a twinkle of playfulness and possibility in my eyes.

Wanna try it too? Find a picture of you as a child. Look at the photo of this younger you and witness the unchanging essence of YOU. The beautiful divine being that deserves unconditional love, compassion, and empathy.

Notice any chatter from your mind and respectively tell it to: ***"ZIP IT"***.

Go to your heart and allow yourself to feel and witness the range of emotions that may or may not come up.

When I did this for the first time, I was met with the most heart-melting of responses from the little girl inside me:

"Really? You love me? Just as I am? I don't have to do anything to make you love me?"

Out poured the tears. I told her I was sorry. I asked for forgiveness.

I thanked her for being patient, told her I loved her, and another layer of healing began.

Your experience with your photo may be similar to or completely different from mine. But isn't it worth a few moments of your time to look at yourself with fresh eyes and show yourself the deep unconditional self-love you deserve?

Perhaps you already are, but there's always more we can do.

Here's a challenge for you: Can you begin to integrate all of this newfound compassion into all areas of your life? Your work, relationships, and even your Yoga practice?

After all, as one of my teachers Eddie Modestini says: *"Yoga is a practice of self-awareness, self-acceptance, and ultimately self-love."*

When I heard Eddie first say this years ago, I understood it. But like many things in Yoga, my understanding of it has gone from grasping a concept to a deep visceral knowing.

My hope is that after this journey together you now also see how this Yoga is potent and transformative in practice on the mat, but even more so in your life.

So let's put this into practice right now. Get a photo of yourself as a child and really look at it. Witness the sweet innocence of you, your magic, your radiance.

Now put both of your hands on the center of your chest and breathe deeply. Breathe as though your breath is moving in and out of the heart space in a slow and steady rhythm.

Visualize yourself as a child standing right in front of you and feel yourself pouring love into that version of yourself. Love yourself the way you craved being loved then. Love and accept yourself the way you want to be now.

Keep breathing. Tears are normal and very healing. Stay for as long as you'd like as you know in every cell of your being that you are Love and that you are deeply Loved as you repeat: **I Am Loving**.

Allow that in and let another layer of self love and healing begin.

Put that photo on your fridge or bathroom mirror. Spend some time with that younger you every day. This is a huge part of your healing and integration of your past, so know that your Saboteurs may attempt to talk you out of it and tell you it's silly. IT IS NOT!

In the end....

As we bring this beautiful experience to an end for now I invite you to reflect back on this crazy story. Can you see now how each chapter of this wild tale has many things to teach you?

Not just about the unique architecture of the iconic Warrior poses, but more importantly about their key qualities and the potent lessons of this ancient practice.

Through the twists and turns of the story I hope it became clear that these invisible tools will help you:

- Learn, evolve, and become even more authentically yourself as you navigate the ups and downs of life and business ownership as gracefully as possible

- Lead with a courageous heart full of love and awareness as you take inspired action while still allowing space for trust and flow

- Take comfort in the fact that you have all the tools you need within you. You simply need to embody and practice them until you truly become them!

It really is a powerful story, isn't it?!

I wasn't joking when I said it would change how you see Yoga, life, and yourself!

I hope you see how the timeless lessons within it will transform you and give you evidence that the seeds of your success already lay within you, you simply need to nurture them. Cultivate them until they blossom out of you with such radiance that they can't be denied by anyone.

However, *no one can do this work for you*. Only you can Wake the Warrior Within you, my beautiful friend. But I'll tell you: when you do you will never be the same. Nor will you want to be.....

Entrepreneurship is certainly not for the faint of heart. So the fact that you're here means you're freaking incredible, so keep up the AH-mazing work!

And until next time....

I am deeply honored and grateful to have been able to share these tools with you. It means SO much to me that you took the time to read this book and if it inspired you in any way it has served its purpose.

Thank you for reading this and for sharing your magic with the world.

Thank you for helping me to fulfill my mission of continuing to elevate the energy of the planet by helping other purpose-driven entrepreneurs and humans to be vibrantly holistically healthy and happy.

With so much love,

P.S.:

Hidden in the tale of Virabhadra are three keys to *fully* unlocking the transformative toolset of Yoga.

Scan the QR code (or go to: https://bit.ly/TWJBsectio n3) below to learn all three, plus learn which one is the most important for you to master to make the inner shifts needed for the outer results you crave!

P.P.S.: If you loved this book please leave a review on Amazon and tell a friend about it!!

More About Megan

As a personal trainer, Yoga instructor, and Positive Intelligence® coach for over 17 years Megan believes that Yoga provides a foundational toolset for lifelong health and wellness.

She has found in her 19 years of practicing Yoga that her experience has evolved from one of focusing just on the physical aspects of the practice to a deeper understanding of who she is and wants to be. Which is why she is SO passionate about helping you put these life changing tools to use in your life so you can be vibrantly holistically healthy and happy! By doing so not only will you feel incredible but you'll be able to get everything done and still have time and energy to enjoy your life.

As an award winning speaker who has shared the virtual stage with Les Brown and Jack Canfield, Megan has been called an influential thought leader by The Los Angeles Tribune. She is a fun and engaging speaker who is available for workshops, keynote speeches and more!

Learn more about Megan and her services here: https://megan-nolan.com/ She is also very active on Instagram where she shares lots of great tips to keep you healthy and funky dance moves to keep you laughing and inspired!

Make sure to follow her there:
https://www.instagram.com/iammegannolan/
(@iammegannolan).

More about the Positive Intelligence®: To learn more about the Saboteurs and the incredible framework of Positive Intelligence® developed by Shirzad Chamine that was mentioned and used throughout the book please see: https://www.positiveintelligence.com/